SPAIN

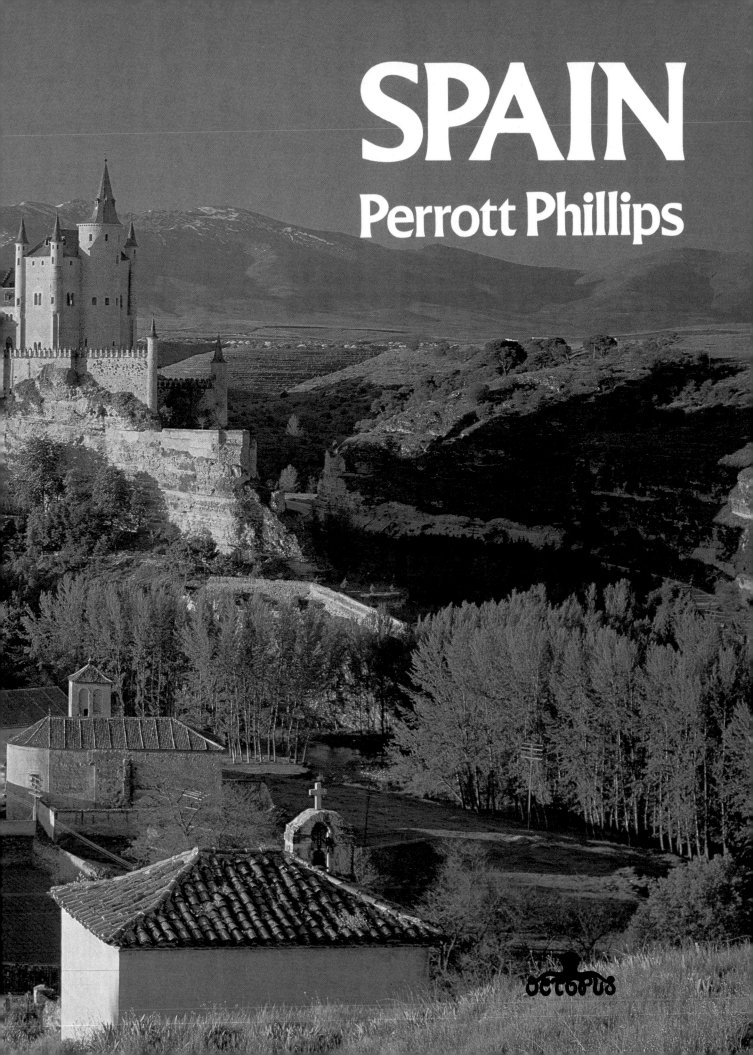

SPAIN
Perrott Phillips

octopus

First published in 1982 by Octopus Books Ltd
59 Grosvenor Street, London W1

© 1982 Octopus Books Limited

ISBN 0 7064 1781 X

Produced by Mandarin Publishers Limited
22a Westlands Road
Quarry Bay, Hong Kong

Printed in Hong Kong

CONTENTS

INTRODUCTION

IT is strange to think that the first package tourists to Spain were the groups of medieval pilgrims who reckoned to wear out three pairs of sandals on the 1100 kilometre (700 mile) trek from the Spanish border to the shrine of Santiago de Compostela. For eleven centuries, pilgrims from all over Europe trudged across northern Spain to reach what was then the most important place of Christian pilgrimage after Jerusalem and Rome. Today, more than 37 million tourists pour into Spain each year, but they probably see less of the country than those early travellers; which must make Spain the best-known, unknown country in the world. It is not the easiest country to explore. Double the size of Britain, it is the most mountainous country in Europe after Switzerland, but there is something for everyone to discover and enjoy. A landscape that varies eccentrically from craggy coasts to lonely swampland where marsh birds cry, from snow-capped peaks, twice the height of anything in Britain, to sun-baked plains as dry as parchment, from the unnerving deserts of Extremadura to the steamy luxuriance of Alicante's palm groves; scenery which has shaped the equally contrasting character of the Spanish people, from aloof Castilian to easy-going Andalucian. There are noble cities, rich with the legacy of Romans and Moors; sleepy townships, where the sand still moves slowly through the hourglass and blindingly whitewashed villages, scattered like sugar cubes down the sides of mountains. The essence of Spain is timelessness. It is not just the atmosphere evoked by ancient stones or places caught in the time-warp of history, it can be the profoundly emotional effect of a great religious ceremony, a local custom that arouses faraway echoes or just the rediscovery of old-fashioned courtesy. This is the real Spain so many holidaymakers seek, yet somehow rarely find. The real Spain where, at one point, you are only thirteen kilometres (eight miles) from Africa.

PAGE 1: A strikingly elegant and colourful couple riding out to a fiesta at Jerez.
PAGES 2 AND 3: Segovia's crowning glory: the fairy-tale Alcázar.
PAGES 4 AND 5: Fresh, juicy oranges from the groves of Majorca in a tempting, wayside display.
BELOW: The ever-receding hills of Andalucia.

CASTLES &
COUNTRYSIDE

I F the map of Spain is like a bull's hide stretched out to dry, then the Guadarrama Mountains form its spinal column, running across the centre in rocky vertebrae. On either side of them are Old and New Castile, named after the numerous castles that loom up like stone mastiffs. Across the whole of Spain, you can see where armies and ideologies have clashed, whether you are looking at the fortresses of feuding kings in Castile and Extremadura or the citadels in the South built and battered in the 781 year war that finally drove out the Moors. There are fortified villages and towns, like the eyrie of **Alquezar** (preceding pages) and haughty Avila, whose 12th century battlements are thrown round the town like a cloak. Great figures strode this way: the Roman Emperors Trajan and Hadrian, Hannibal, El Cid, Ferdinand and Isabella, Christopher Columbus, Ignatius Loyola, even Don Quixote, whose windmills still whir on the plains of La Mancha. Time has made few changes to the vast and varied countryside. There are wheatfields like sheets of gold leaf; mountain peaks that rear up more than 3,500 metres (11,600 feet); stretches of desolate scrubland, where even the birds have fled from the sun; woodland streams trembling with trout; hillside terraced in vines and vast, rolling olive groves.

Castles are the great milestones of Spain. They seem to crown almost every hill, peering suspiciously across the surrounding countryside. Over the centuries, they have shuddered under sieges and bombardments; changing hands only after vast ransoms, loveless marriages, oceans of blood, broken bodies or ruined reputations. In 1185, the castle of **Alarcón** (below left) in the province of Cuenca, was besieged for a year. King Alfonso VIII had almost given up hope of taking the fortress when his commander, Fernan de Ceballos, suggested a daring idea. Using two swords like mountaineers' pitons, Ceballos scaled the walls at the head of an assault group, attacking from behind and claiming victory over the exhausted defenders.

Becalmed now in a sea of poppies, Alarcón no longer repels invaders. It is one of around 80 historic buildings, including many castles and fortresses, which have been converted into luxurious, government-run hotels, called Paradors. Sited in some of Spain's most spectacular and unspoiled areas, they transform into vivid reality the pipedream of 'a castle in Spain'. But it is not just the idea of 'living like a king' that draws more than half a million people each year to the Paradors. It is the chance of touching the hem of history.

You can stand on the battlements of the Parador of Conde de Gondomar at the very spot where, in 1493, the people of Bayona saw Columbus sail on his way to discover the new world. Whilst as you walk under the great gateway of the castle-Parador at Zafra, you are following the youthful footsteps of Hernan Cortes, the soldier who conquered Mexico with a handful of men. At the fortress of Jarandilla de la Vera, you can stay at the last stopping-place of Emperor Charles V. He stayed there in 1555 before embracing seclusion and death at the nearby monastery of Yuste. And if you go to Ciudad Rodrigo you can look down from the tower and imagine the troops of the Duke of Wellington cutting hidden zigzag trenches up the hill towards the walls, as they did in the siege and capture of the castle in 1812.

Some castles have fallen more peacefully. A signpost in a remote corner of south-west Spain points to the village of Castellar. Eight kilometres (5 miles) further on, and 245 metres (800 feet) above sea level, you arrive at a castle on a hilltop, but there is no sign of the village. The reason is that it is locked inside the tenth century walls of the great fortress. Over the years, as the castle fell into disrepair, the villagers moved in and built their houses within the battlements.

No cosy community disturbs the eerie calm of the **castle of Belmonte** (right), built by Don Juan Pacheco in 1456, and which guards the southern fringes of the vast central plain of La Mancha. Although still privately owned, Belmonte is now deserted like many castles in Spain, impossible to live in or maintain. The caretaker toils up from the village to take you round the sentry walks, explain the extraordinary optical effects of the wooden Moorish ceilings – still in perfect condition – and show you the dungeon. Its only entrance is a tiny hole through which prisoners were lowered on a 12 metre (40 ft) rope, never to be hauled up again.

Fray Luis de León, one of Spain's greatest thinkers,

was born in the village. In 1572, while teaching at Salamanca University, he was betrayed to the Inquisition and jailed on a false charge of heresy. He remained in prison for five years before being allowed to return to the work he loved. On his first morning back, a silent and nervous crowd of professors and students watched him mount his dais, waiting for a bitter attack on those who had betrayed him. Fray Luis smiled at the crowd and began, 'As we were saying yesterday . . .' picking up at exactly the point where his lesson had been cut short five years earlier.

In keeping with that stoical element which is an essential part of their character – and demonstrated so clearly by Fray Luis – the Spanish have built fortresses, even towns, in the most desolate and inaccessible places. The houses of **Cuenca** (below), on the banks of the Júcar and Huécar rivers, are thrust into space. They seem to be poised only momentarily before disintegrating and tumbling 150 metres (500 feet) down a sheer rock face. The famous *Casas Colgadas*, or Hanging Houses, of this strange town have been literally keeping the townsfolk in suspense for more than 200 years. They ran out of ground space long ago and since the town was perched on a precipice, the only way to build was upwards, piling one room on

another like children's bricks. Wedged side by side, some of the older buildings are 12 storeys high, but still only the width of a single room. Incredibly, not one has ever collapsed. The precipitous nature of life in Cuenca has influenced a whole school of abstract painters whose work – often stark and severe – is displayed in a museum set in three adjoining cliffside houses.

It is not art, however, which sends thousands of people scurrying down to the fields below the town in autumn, each one carrying a delicate, camelhair brush. Cuenca is the saffron centre of the world and the brushes are to help remove the golden pollen which will later end up as a vital ingredient in many a paella in the faraway tourist Costas.

In the Rioja a different kind of bloom has brought industry and wealth to the area; the noble bloom of the grape. These 5000 square kilometres (1800 square miles), a green-gold mosaic of terraced vineyards and cornfields, have been producing Spain's finest wines since 1102. They were known even to the medieval pilgrims who crossed the bridge at **Puente de la Reina** (above) – built by Queen Urraca in 1085 – on their way to Santiago de Compostela. In northern Spain the sun is more merciful than it is in the middle. Everywhere is ripeness. The *vegas*, or market gardens, burst with peaches, peppers, tomatoes and aubergines. Roebuck and wild boar roam the mountain slopes. Quail, partridge and redwing flock overhead. The rivers are dappled with trout and they catch crayfish in baskets baited with entrails.

Northern Spain is as green as Galway, as sheer as Switzerland, as fertile as France. Parallel with the coast, the Cantabrian mountains unfold for 650 kilometres (400 miles) in an emerald curtain, rising to 2,600 metres (8,600 ft) at the Picos de Europa. Here tweed-clad Spaniards carrying London-made guns hunt bears, wolves, fleet-footed chamois and the elusive ibex.

It is also wet. 'The rain in Spain stays mainly in the plain' may be a reliable way of improving one's vowels but it is no use as a weather forecast. The rain stays mainly here in northern Spain. The ancient, galleried farmhouses, lying well back in lush, green fields, have

a permanent hook outside the door for the family umbrella. Their balconies, called *miradores*, are enclosed in glass; a style which achieves its most elegant reflection in **La Coruña** (below), in the extreme north-west corner, where the average annual rainfall is 165 cm (66 in). Just 55 cm (22 in) more than London. Piled on top of each other like a display cabinet, the balconies have earned La Coruña the name of 'The city of glass'.

This muscular area, so different from the conventional 'travel poster' image, makes one wonder, not for the first time, what *is* the 'real Spain'? Certainly not the Basque country, near the western end of the French border; the home of the oldest and most enigmatic of all the Iberian peoples. The short, thickset, bullet-headed Basques are unique. They are hearty eaters and devoted to energetic games. Their race is a mystery to ethnologists and their language, Euskera, a cat's cradle of z's and x's, is a riddle to philologists. Their fast-moving *jai allai* is an exclusive Basque game, their stone *caserios*, Alpine-like farmhouses, are found nowhere else in Spain and their ability to chop through an oak log in four blows and dance gingerly on the edge of a glass of wine without spilling a drop are inimitable Basque

feats. Basque farmers still plough with teams of yoked oxen and scythe pocket-handkerchief meadows by hand. On the coast, they set out from brightly-coloured, toytown harbours to net vast catches of sardines, tunny, hake and squid . . . fish as bright as newly-minted coins.

But for Spain's most adventurous seafarers, we must move far to the west. To where the coast turns into a disorientated Norway, with deep fjords called *rías* clawing into the rock. To **Galicia** (overleaf). Here, the misty land looks as if it were lost in the 16th century. The westernmost tip points to what was once thought to be the edge of the world, where the sun went down. It was known in Latin as *finis terra* – the end of the earth – and we call it Cape Finisterre. The Romans left another legacy, the slate-slabbed walls and bastions which completely encircle the city of Lugo. They are so perfectly preserved, you can walk right round the city on top of them.

Galicia and its seagoing people trace their origins back to the Celts. They have blue eyes and fair hair, play the bagpipes, dance a form of reel and eat something suspiciously like porridge. The women wear clumpish clogs known as *zuecos* and their men build strange barns on stilts called *horreos*. Again, they are

the complete antithesis of the conventional Spaniard, underlining this difference by seeming to spend more time away from their homeland than in it. They are the great wanderers of Spain and in many countries of South America the name Gallego, or Galician, still signifies 'Spaniard'. Or do they perhaps descend from the ancient Norsemen? Certainly the blood-curdling cry of the Galician folk singer, the silent blue-eyed fishermen staring at the sea, the long curved prow of the fishing *dorna*, all seem to echo the days when Vikings prowled the coastal towns of Galicia.

But Galicia is the birthplace of an even greater mystery. One evening, in the early 9th century, a hermit named Pelagius saw an unknown star in the sky. This vision, said to have been accompanied by 'celestial music', led him to a stone tomb containing three bodies. One of them was of St James the Apostle, whose remains were believed to have arrived in Spain aboard a boat, been buried and then forgotten. The King of the Asturias, Alfonso II, immediately visited the tomb, pronounced the remains genuine and declared St James Protector of Spain. Round the field of the star – *campus stellae*, later corrupted to Compostela – arose a city, a cathedral and a legend.

According to the story, a vision of St James, mounted on a white charger, appeared at the Battle of Clavijo in the ninth century and helped the Spanish troops to defeat the Moors. The saint became Santiago Matamoros, St James the Moor-slayer, and by the 17th century had apparently come to the aid of the Christians at least forty times. The 11th century cathedral containing the remains of the saint, became the most important place of Christian pilgrimage after Jerusalem and Rome. The golden age was the 13th century, when between 500,000 and two million

pilgrims a year plodded across northern Spain at the rate of sixteen kilometres (ten miles) a day to the holy shrine.

They were a motley crowd, ranging from the genuinely devout to criminals who had been sentenced to 'Five years in chains or a pilgrimage to St James'. Peasants rubbed shoulders with princes. Bishops strode side by side with battle-scarred soldiers. Some turned the journey into a kind of holiday, while others endured it as a form of penance. The columns were often attacked by bandits and they were easy prey for thieves, tricksters, unscrupulous innkeepers and dishonest guides. Bands of pious knights pledged themselves to protect the pilgrims on the way and in 1130 the world's first 'guidebook' circulated among the weary marchers. It was by the French priest, Aymery Picaud, and painted a discouraging picture of the danger and hardships ahead, with grudging advice on good resting places and hospitable inns. The people of Navarre came off particularly badly. 'They are perverse, perfidious, disloyal, corrupted, voluptuous, expert in every violence, cruel and quarrelsome', he wrote, adding 'and any one of them would murder a pilgrim for a sou.' Some pilgrims, however, could give as good as they got. One could never tell who was concealed under the traditional pilgrim garb of heavy woollen robe and undershirt, wide-brimmed hat, water gourd, heavy stave and belt of scallop shells – the emblem of St James. According to legend, the Emperor Charlemagne visited the shrine in 778, followed by King Alfonso II, El Cid, Louis VII of France, St Francis of Assisi and James III of Scotland. To keep up their spirits, some pilgrims bored holes in their staves, so that they could play them like flutes. On they tramped, following the Pilgrim's Route – the Milky Way, they called it – from Pamplona to

Logroño, Santo Domingo de la Calzada to Burgos, León to Ponferrada and finally Villafranca to Santiago itself.

At the end was an indulgence from the Pope, a free pardon for criminals or maybe just a certificate to prove you had completed the gruelling journey. And gruelling it was, for the chances of dying on the way were high. Aymery Picaud even accused the northern Spaniards of poisoning the water in the wells and streams. The idea, said Picaud darkly, was to render the pilgrims insensible, so that they could be murdered and robbed. Many a penitent must have dropped his water gourd in terror on reading Picaud's warning. It probably gave rise to the whole myth about 'Don't drink the water in Spain'. At Estella, on the other hand, Picaud praised the water as 'sweet and excellent' and in the style of a modern good food guide went on to recommend the local bread, wine, fish and meat. **Estella** (left) is still an enchanting

town. Franciscan monks wander down the streets shopping and the cliff-like backs of old houses are mirrored in the River Ega, the source of Picaud's thirst-quenching water.

One of the biggest resting-places on the way to Santiago was Santo Domingo de la Calzada, where the pilgrims' hospice – which has been receiving guests since 1216 – has been converted into another government-run Parador. In the old days, the pilgrims had to make do with a straw palliasse, crude wine, bread and whey. Now visitors live in three-star luxury, with huge double rooms containing serve-yourself refrigerators full of drinks, a comfortable lounge and a great, beamed dining hall. Yet parts of the village have not changed for centuries and the ancient bell tower opposite the inn chimes the hours with all the tunefulness of a cracked cup.

For those not restricted to a penitential diet, northern Spain's abundant countryside, coupled with its long, rocky coastline, produces the most varied cuisine in the country. 'Look for a restaurant run by women', say the connoisseurs, 'they are always best.' The menu is likely to include delicious game from the forests, fat trout from the rivers, tender baby lamb, stupendous stews, huge prawns, succulent vegetables and the finest wines in Spain's cellars, the clean-limbed whites and robust reds from the **Rioja vineyards** (near left).

No wonder the old pilgrims found a final burst of energy to clamber up the last hill on their journey, to see the spires of Santiago shimmering below them. According to custom, the first man to the top shouted 'My Joy!' and was elected 'King' of the group by the others. Thousands of people called King, Konig, Leroy or Rex owe their names to some energetic ancestor.

Pilgrims of a sort still flock to northern Spain. The Spanish prefer the temperate climate for their own holidays, sunning themselves in little harbour-resorts like Lequeitio, Ondarroa, Castro Urdiales, Llanes or **Bermeo** (below), one of the most colourful fishing ports in Spain, where the masts of the tunny boats look like a forest of cocktail sticks. Desperate to escape from the kiln of Madrid, even the Spanish Civil Service moves with unaccustomed speed each summer as it moves lock, stock and red tape to the Cantabrian resort of San Sebastián, earning it the nickname 'Madrid-on-Sea'. And for those travellers who still heed the call of St James, there is the evocative experience of entering one of the pokey little shops behind the cathedral and buying souvenirs identical to those pilgrims brought back centuries ago: small, silver scallop shells, the emblem of Santiago Matamoros, the patron saint of Spain.

He is the patron saint, too, of the Spanish conquest of South America. For the *conquistadores*, who carved out the greatest empire the world had ever seen with the blades of their swords went into battle shouting the same old cry, *'Santiago y cierra España!'* (Up Spaniards and at them!). To appreciate the inherited stoicism of men like Cortes, Pizarro and Balboa, one only has to travel to their birthplace, the rough, earthy and desolate region of Extremadura.

It is a wild land of eagles' nests, vast uncultivated spaces, brief wooded areas, dour people and taciturn towns built round ancient manor houses. Even now you have to be hardy to toil in this sun-creased terrain where the farmers pray for just a few drops of the rain that falls so generously on the head of St James at Compostela. Many of the palaces in the venerable hill town of Trujillo were built with the gold from the Indes and the sandstone crests carved on the walls of the 15th and 16th century mansions in Cáceres are of noble families who fought and died in the Americas.

The *conquistadores* did not necessarily fight for reasons of conscience, through religious fervour or even for plain loot; they fought because there was precious little else to do. The arid sierras and bleak plains of Extremadura could not support them. Extremadura is still one of the most underpopulated regions of Spain and in soporific little towns like Zafra, you can wander through a Plaza Mayor as

silent as a cathedral cloister, with barely a dog for company. Just behind the square is Zafra Castle, built in 1437 and once the stronghold of the Duke of Feria. The Duke was among the grandees in attendance on Philip II of Spain when he went to England to marry Mary Tudor; yet another of those odd and unexpected links between the ruling dynasties of the two countries. While in England, the Duke married Jane Dormer, Mary's best friend, and brought her back to Spain. To Jane, anything Spanish was the next thing to perfection and she even managed to absorb the morbid Spanish attitude to death. After her husband died, she kept her own coffin in the castle to remind her of mortality and she hung a tiny skull on her rosary.

Hernan Cortes, the conqueror of Mexico, was a friend of the Ferias and a frequent visitor to the castle. Which is why it was renamed the Parador Hernan Cortes when the government converted it to a sumptuous hotel in 1968. It is a finer monument to the great *conquistador* than the rather ugly statue which stands in the Plaza Mayor in his birthplace, the village of Medellin. As dusty and forgotten as any place in Extremadura, Medellin has inherited nothing of the unprecedented wealth won by her most distinguished son. Extremadura as a whole gained little from the monumental plunder of the Americas. Gold by the galleon-load arrived from Mexico and Peru, only to be frittered away on useless military campaigns and the shoring up of a ramshackle and rebellious empire in Austria, Germany, Italy and the Low Countries. Yet, like some Lost World, Extremadura has a fascination all of its own. Deserted **Garrovillas** (left), from which all the young people have fled to find work elsewhere, would not be the same with its rickety Plaza Mayor crowded with tourists. And the lack of industrial development has preserved wonderful places like Mérida, which the Romans knew in 25 B.C. as Emerita Augustus.

One searing afternoon, as the storks rested sensibly in their nests, I trudged through Mérida's dusty streets to the Roman ruins on the outskirts of the town. The heat struck back from the terraces of the amphitheatre, making the stones bleach the eyes. I descended into the underground dressing-room, which was cool, dark and so ghostly that one could almost hear the excited chatter of the Roman actors as they prepared to go on. Up a few steps to the stage . . . then the sunlight struck me like the blade of a sword and there before me were the rising tiers, just as the first actor on the stage must have seen them, when they were filled with an expectant audience, eight centuries before the birth of Christ.

One of the reasons why endless tracts of land remained uncultivated in Extremadura for nearly 500 years was that they were owned by the powerful and ruthless Guild of Sheepowners – the *Mesta* – who used them for grazing. Only gentlemen, like the lords of **Mombeltran castle** (below), were allowed to join the *Mesta* and they enjoyed special privileges from successive kings. Farmers had to allow the sheep to pass through their fields and in one year, more than $1\frac{1}{2}$ million Merino sheep were allowed to roam across the region, destroying everything in their path. Immense flocks still graze on the **Extremaduran plateau** (overleaf) in winter but in the summer they are driven into the cooler and greener hills.

For you cannot move far in Spain without climbing upwards and we are now on the edge of the craggy sierras which lumber across every horizon. Bordering the central plain of La Mancha, where Don Quixote tilted at the windmills, is the 550 kilometre (350 mile) mountain wall of the Sierra Nevada, the rooftop of Spain.

From the 3,555 metre (11,663 ft) summit of Mount Mulhacén – nearly three times higher than Ben Nevis – the foothills winnow away beneath you as far as the

southern coast. Piercing blue gentians pattern the ground like an expensive carpet and the air is aromatic with the scent of wild sage. The only sounds are cowbells echoing in the valleys and, if you are lucky, a shepherd boy singing a *copla*, or verse, his reedy voice carried in the thin air until it vanishes like a wraith among the distant peaks. **Whitewashed villages** (right) cling to the slopes like intrepid mountaineers and, above the snowline, strange lakes appear, as blue as a Viking's eye. One of them is called La Laguna de Vácares, known to the mountain people as *El Ojo del Mar*, the Eye of the Sea. They believe it is linked to the Mediterranean by a series of underground caverns. Local legend tells of a beautiful woman with an insatiable appetite for men, who lives in a Moorish castle beneath its still waters, waiting to drag unwary travellers into the depths. Even now, no shepherd lingers near the edge after sunset.

I once rode across the Sierra Nevada on horseback, stopping at *posadas*, almost medieval muleteers' inns, where everyone slept all together in one room above the horses. Everything seemed to be scaled down to fit the short, stocky mountain folk. The ceilings were low, you cracked your head on the door frames, the mirrors were hung at waist level, your feet stuck out of the bedclothes and the rush-seated chairs looked like cast-outs from the nursery. I felt like Gulliver blundering about in Lilliput. Most bedrooms had a distorting mirror, an instantly collapsible coatrack on the wall, a ewer and basin you filled from the horse trough and brass-knobbed beds with mattresses stuffed with straw or knobbly pieces of foam rubber. In one, when I genteelly enquired the direction of the toilet, the landlord replied in astonishment, 'Toilet? You go with your horse!'.

It was a far cry from the Paradors. The caves of **Guadix** (below), near Granada in Andalucia, were an even further cry. As you approach, huge sandstone cliffs and pillars, eroded by nature into bizarre shapes, rear above your head. In the blowtorch heat, a haze of pinkish dust hovers between the walls of the gullies

and canyons and it is not until you are right on top of them that you realise they are *alive*, like a termites' nest. Guadix is a village of troglodytes, or cave dwellers. Thousands of them live in caverns scooped out from the sandstone. There are streets of caves with nameplates and numbers on the doors. There are cave taverns, cave shops and cave schools. Only a few of them are primitive slums. Some have telephones, nearly all boast a television and if you want to extend your home there is no problem; you merely hack out another couple of rooms.

Of all the southern ranges, the **Sierra Alpujarras** (overleaf) was until recently the most unknown and inaccessible, enfolding almost lost hamlets like **Jerez de Marquesada** (inset, overleaf). The village of Yegen was once so isolated that, before World War Two, archeologists were baffled by reports that rare Punic and Iberian coins were still being used as day-to-day currency. It turned out that an old villager had died leaving a hoard of them in a drawer and his sons, not knowing any better, spent the lot. Nobody had bothered to look at them closely and they were only recognized when an astonished British visitor got a

handful in his change. Some of them are now in the Ashmolean Museum, Oxford. At Trevelez – the highest village in Spain, and proud of its snow-cured hams – older villagers even now believe that the hams are visited and 'blessed' by *hechiceras*, or witches, who fly by night over the sierras. Flying is probably the easiest way to see the Alpujarras, once described as 'the secret attic of Spain'.

Not surprisingly, castles are thin on the ground in this inhospitable terrain, which allows the castle of Calahorra – 'besieged' by Charlton Heston in the movie, *El Cid* – to make an even more dramatic impact than usual. It lowers over the countryside, alone, immense, impregnable. Yet it has a heart of gold. Hidden behind the forbidding walls is a perfectly preserved Renaissance palace. The exquisite courtyard is in two storeys, the balustrades and pillars delicately sculpted from Carrara marble in 1510. Magnificent coats of arms are carved above the doors and a monumental staircase leads to the watchtowers and sentry-walks. Calahorra's walls echo with life and laughter. For it is the playground of all the local children, a real life fairytale palace in which to play.

It is one of the biggest castles in Spain, rivalling the whitestone bulk of Penafiel, which looks like a stranded ship, square at the stern and pointed at the bow. **Penafiel** (left) was started in 1307 and – at 200 metres (220 yards) long and 20 metres (22 yards) wide – is still an awe-inspiring monument to feudal power.

But at **Ronda** (above) – 700 metres (2,300 feet) up in the southern sierras – nature has carved out her own awesome and impregnable fortress. Ronda is a town where the ground has been cut away from under your feet. It is perched on either side of a ravine 275 metres (900 feet) deep – the Tajo gorge – and as recently as 1945 was still a retreat for mountain bandits. The two halves of the town are linked by a vertiginous bridge which took nearly 40 years to build and cost the life of architect José Martín de Aldihuela, who plunged to his death while inspecting the works in 1761. The bridge is only 70 metres (230 feet) long and the views into the gorge from the heavily-grilled parapet are terrifying.

Ronda is an alarming place, which may explain why its history is corroded with cruelty and littered with corpses. In the 14th century, the Moorish ruler, Abd el Malik, ordered 365 steps to be cut into the Tajo's sheer stone face, leading to a water reserve at the bottom of the gorge. Dozens fell to their death during the work. And when Abd el Malik sent down Christian slaves to haul up the water in skin bags, many found the work so back-breaking that they committed suicide the same way. Another Moorish despot, Al Mutadid Ibn Abbad, invited influential people he suspected of treachery to a dinner. Afterwards, they were shown to the *hammam* – the Arab baths – where they were clubbed senseless by hidden guards and then walled in to die of suffocation. On the lip of the gorge, the Casa del Rey Moro was once the home of King Badis, who used to drink wine from the jewel-encrusted skulls of his victims and in the 18th century, prisoners huddled in a cell right inside the bridge before being heaved into the ravine.

The cell has now been converted into a little restaurant where tourists sip beer, watch the birds wheeling in the ravine beneath their feet and ponder on how a town ever came to be built in such an impossible place. Sheer magic or sheer madness? Either way, utterly Spanish.

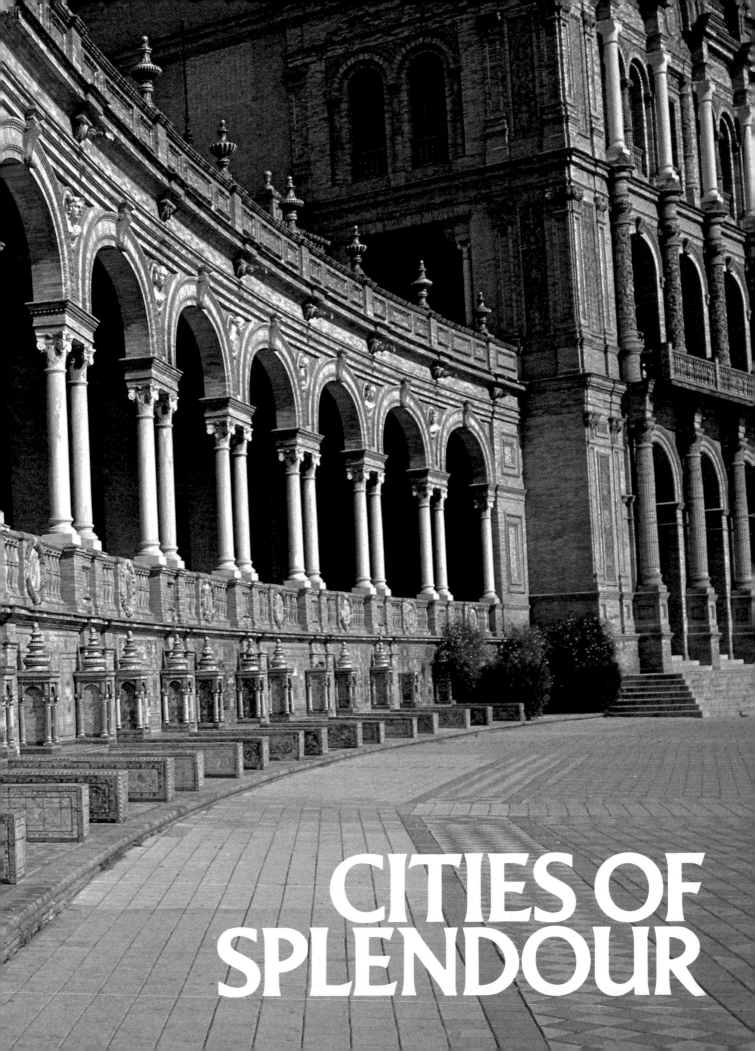

CITIES OF SPLENDOUR

THE cities of Spain are glorious and not just because of their architectural grandeur: no two are alike in their mood, let alone appearance. They even seem to *look* in different directions. Madrid's attention is invariably focused on itself. Barcelona gazes enviously across to France. The languorous Moslem cities of Seville, Granada and Córdoba forever glance backwards to the Moors, whilst the cathedral-dominated cities of Burgos and Santiago seem to gaze upwards, like supplicants to Heaven. Not surprisingly, the people of Madrid believe that everything revolves around the capital. Kilometre 'O', from which all distances are measured, stands in the bustling Puerta del Sol. So does the clock which sets standard time throughout the country. If Madrid is the centre of Spanish bureaucracy, then Barcelona is the commercial hub. Though even her hard-headed businessmen have time for fantasy. In the centre of Barcelona is a futuristic cathedral of bizarre appearance, still unfinished after 55 years. Indeed, each city has its flight of imagination on a monumental scale. Seville has a cathedral so huge that the city fathers boasted, 'The world will say we were mad!'; Granada has the Moorish Alhambra built to create paradise on earth and Córdoba has its cathedral hidden *inside* a mosque. Cities of splendour, all of them.

For centuries, alchemists searched for the legendary Philosopher's Stone that turned base metal into gold. Seville went one better. It turned gold into stone. For over 200 years, the gold of the Americas poured into the city, which was at that time the hub of the Spanish-American empire. Every ship to and from the New World had to register in Seville and, although the city was 80 kilometres (50 miles) inland from the south-west coast, galleons sailed up the Guadalquivir river and unloaded their cargoes of silver, gold, spices and tobacco in front of the twelve-sided Tower of Gold, built in 1220 by the Moors and named after its glinting, gold-faced tiles. Seville transmuted its share of those riches into buildings that are still stunning with their combination of confidence, elegance and magnificence.

Confidence was something the Sevillanos had even before the 'gold rush' started. When the old Moorish mosque was demolished in 1401, work began on **Seville's new cathedral** (preceding pages). It took 100 years to complete and is the third largest in the world, after St Peter's in Rome and St Paul's in London.

The Spanish are fond of quoting its statistics: 117 metres (383 feet) long by 76 metres (251 feet) wide, with an interior of 510,000 cubic metres (18 million cubic feet); 40 pillars, some reaching to 56 metres (184 feet), supporting a ceiling with 69 vaults; 74 stained glass windows, nine doors and the biggest altarpiece in the world, a masterpiece of late 15th century Flemish carving and gilding, 20 metres (65 feet) high and 13 metres (43 feet) wide. But these pocket-calculator figures give no idea of the breathtaking beauty of the interior, with its exuberant wood carvings and sculpture, its decorations as glittering as the gold of the Incas. There are also unexpectedly intimate touches. Twice a year, ten young boys in satin knee-breeches, buckled shoes and plumed hats perform a stately minuet in front of the high altar to the sound of castanets. Pope Eugenius IV allowed the dance to continue only as long as the costumes would last. They have been repatched so often that barely a shred of the original remains.

Fifty Christian Masses are said each day in the cathedral, yet the bell that summons the faithful to prayer rings out from a heathen minaret. When they destroyed the mosque, the Sevillanos couldn't bear to include the lovely **Giralda Tower** (below). It was built in 1184 and is identical to the Koutoubia minaret in Marrakesh. The gradually-ascending ramp inside makes the 93 metre (304 ft) climb easy, thanks to Ibn Yussuf, who had it built that way so he could ride up on his horse to view the city.

Despite its exotically Moorish appearance, the Alcázar Palace would not have been one of the buildings surveyed so proudly by Ibn Yussuf. It was built in the 14th century by Pedro the Cruel. But Arab habits and customs had so penetrated the life of Christian Spain (and still persist) that Pedro borrowed Moorish craftsmen from Granada to give his palace the authentic touch. It was the bizarre custom in the court for gallants to curry favour by drinking the bathwater of Pedro's mistress. When one wit declined the drink on the ground that 'Having tasted the sauce,

he might covet the partridge', Pedro the Cruel lived up to his name and beheaded him.

Seville has a languorous, eastern air of which Santiago de Compostela in the north-west of Spain would no doubt totally disapprove. In Santiago's sternly dramatic **cathedral** (right) lie the remains of St James the Moor-slayer, locked in a silver casket beneath the high altar. With its sculpted façades, bas-reliefs, images in jasper, alabaster and marble, the cathedral is in effect the world's biggest reliquary. Since the beginning of the 9th century, pilgrims have made their way to Santiago to venerate the relics – even when they weren't there. When Sir Francis Drake attacked La Coruña in 1589, the bishop took

the call to prayer from a minaret of corpses.'

Strange, then, to find a statue of a Moor in a place of honour in the cathedral of Toledo, for 500 years the capital of Christian Spain. Toledo is centrally placed 70 kilometres (44 miles) south of Madrid. When Alfonso VI captured Toledo in 1085, he promised the Moslem ruler, Abu Walid, that the mosque would be respected. But no sooner was the king's back turned than troops under the command of the Queen and the Archbishop of Toledo burst into the mosque and desecrated it. The king was so furious that he threatened to execute the soldiers and burn the bishop at the stake. With remarkable magnanimity, Abu Walid interceded and saved their lives. When the mosque was finally pulled down and the cathedral built on its site nearly 150 years later, the humane Moor was placed among the saints.

The seat of the Primate of Spain, Toledo Cathedral is one of the wonders of Christendom. The great reredos which rises high above the altar was carved between 1502–1503 and, like some heavenly dolls' house, contains 14 compartments showing scenes from the New Testament. The figures at the top are much

the relics to a place of safety and promptly lost them. They were not rediscovered until 1879. Meanwhile the pilgrims still came, by tradition touching a central pillar in the Portico de la Gloria as they entered, so that over the centuries the carving has worn as smooth as glass.

On great religious occasions, the *botafumeiro* – a 2 metre (6 ft) high, silver-plated censer – is swung right across the width of the nave on the end of a steel cable. Eight men haul on the rope as the *botafumeiro* flies up to the heights of the vaulted roof before plunging down like an express train over the heads of the congregation, trailing incense and sparks from the charcoal blazing inside. It is an unnerving sight and one cannot blame worshippers whose faith starts to desert them as the immense vessel thunders towards them like a bomb. Once, the *botafumeiro* got out of control and hurtled through a stained glass window into the plaza outside.

Unlike most Spanish cathedrals, Santiago is bordered by plazas on all sides. The inside of Santiago Cathedral, however, is no exception to the general rule that Spanish cathedrals are dark and gloomy. But León Cathedral seems to have wandered in from another country. All is lightness and grace, the stone floors a rainbow of reflections from the spectacular **stained glass windows** (above) representing every style from the 13th century onwards. More than half the cathedral's wall surface is glass. There are 125 arched windows, some as high as nine metres (30 feet), rising in multicoloured tiers; 57 circular ones and three gigantic roses. As the vivid Spanish light streams through, visitors are stained all the colours of the spectrum by these stupendous 'coloured slides' of Christendom, telling the story of saints, sinners, martyrs, miracles and all the wonders of the Gospel.

León was attacked by the Moors in 996 and after a year's siege the merciless Al-Mansur – 'The Scourge of Christendom' – destroyed the town and nearly all its inhabitants. 'His muezzins', said one historian, 'gave bigger than those on the lower levels, giving the illusion that they are all the same size. The famous Transparente Altar of 1732 is a rollicking baroque confection of gilded cherubs, crests, swags and curlicues illuminated by a shaft of light from a skylight in the roof.

The biscuit-coloured city of **Toledo** (below), almost strangled in a loop of the River Tagus, has changed little since El Greco painted it in the 16th century. Tucked away in streets as narrow as a knife are a recreation of the artist's studio in a period house and the church of St Tomas, which contains his masterpiece, the *Burial of Count Orgaz*. The group of sombre grandees shown in the painting contains one interloper. The sixth figure from the left is a self-portrait of El Greco himself.

Dominating the skyline of Toledo is the Alcázar fortress, a squat and bulky building with four towers, like an inverted table. Destroyed and rebuilt countless times, the Alcázar is described by the historian Fernando Chueca Goitia as 'one of the most unfortunate and ill-fated buildings in Spain'. In 1936, during the Civil War, it was the scene of a heartrending incident. Besieged within the building with a handful of soldiers and 600 women and children, the Commander was told on the telephone that troops of the Workers' Militia had captured his son. Colonel José Moscardo was given ten minutes to surrender the garrison, otherwise his son would be shot. He was allowed to speak to the boy on the telephone and the poignant conversation that followed is displayed in more than 20 languages in the Colonel's room in the Alcázar, preserved just as it was at that moment:

Papa!

What is happening, son?

They say they are going to shoot me if you do not surrender.

Then commend your soul to God, shout VIVA ESPAÑA! and VIVO CRISTO REY! and die like a hero.

A very strong kiss, papa.

Goodbye, my son, a very strong kiss.

On August 23, Luis Moscardo, aged 16, was taken out and shot. The Alcázar was relieved exactly four weeks later.

Even the Toledanos admit their city possesses a strange atmosphere – aloof, withdrawn, mystical – and it has been described as an oriental island marooned in the centre of Spain. In total contrast, the great seaport of Barcelona in the north-east is regarded as Spain's most European city. The cosmopolitan, hardworking and prosperous citizens have no time for introspection. Their gaze is forever outwards, across the Pyrenees to France. The Counts of Barcelona once ruled a territory which straddled the Pyrenees and for three centuries the city shared commercial supremacy of the Mediterranean with Venice. The Catalans are proud of their business sense and regard themselves as the mainstay of Spain. It is no coincidence that their most highly prized characteristic is *seny* – or commonsense – and that the main station in the busy seaport is called the Estación de Francia.

From his tall column, the figure of **Christopher Columbus** (above) looks down on the cargo vessels as they edge into the harbour, past a reconstruction of the Santa María, the caravel in which he sailed to America in 1492. On his return, Columbus brought with him some American Indians, who were baptized in Barcelona Cathedral before an astonished crowd. The flower-filled and tree-shaded Ramblas – with its cafés, bookstalls, birdcages and unending promenade of strollers – leads from the seaport to the centre of town. It passes the Barrio Chino, a maze of narrow, sooty, slightly sinister alleys which were once one of the most dangerous 'thieves' kitchens' in Europe.

Though daydreaming is not part of the down-to-earth Catalan character, Barcelona boasts the most fantastical building in the whole of Christendom. The four steeples of the Cathedral of La Familia Sagrada, designed by the controversial architect, Antonio Gaudí, crane over the city's rooftops like giraffes. It is not until you reach the building that you realise it is only half-finished. The cathedral aroused bitter controversy from the moment the first stone was laid. Its weird, surrealist façade is covered in every kind of decoration. Carved vines writhe up the walls, a flock of stone chickens peck above the main door and the sun glints on pieces of ceramic, glass and brightly coloured tiles. There is not a straight line in the whole structure, the windows are cave-like holes, the eaves drip and bubble like molten lava and the bottle-shaped spires are tipped with what look like outsize billiard balls. The cathedral will probably remain an uncompleted masterpiece, a tantalizing reminder of what might have been. Antonio Gaudí was killed in a street accident in 1925 with the plans forever locked in his head.

Even far-off Barcelona suffered under the hands of Al-Mansur, who left the city in ashes in 985. Yet Al-Mansur was no barbarian. Under his rule, the city of Córdoba in the centre of southern Spain became the cultural and intellectual centre of the western world. While the rest of Europe was dragging itself on all fours through the Dark Ages, Córdoba boasted more than one million inhabitants. There were over 300 mosques, public baths, palaces – even a public library – within its stone walls. Physicists, doctors, astronomers, mathematicians and philosophers flocked to the city to share their knowledge and wisdom.

Its supreme glory was the Great Mosque, built by Abd-er-Rahman in 786 and enlarged by Al-Mansur until it covered 23,000 square metres (250,000 square feet) of the city. Revenge is bitter, rather than sweet. In 1523, King Carlos I carelessly sanctioned a plan to build a Christian cathedral right in the middle of the mosque. Although the Cordobans were outraged – and the local authorities issued an edict threatening death to anyone working on the cathedral – the plan went ahead. When Carlos actually set eyes on the hopelessly incongruous structure in 1526, he exploded, 'What you have made here, you can find anywhere. What you have destroyed is to be found nowhere else in the world!' Even now, the 850 exquisitely-beautiful pillars and the striped red-and-white arches of the original mosque – like a forest full of zebras – fascinate visitors more than the cathedral crouching in the centre. Whichever way you look, you get the same **arcaded view** (below); like some Arabian Nights conjuring trick with mirrors.

Córdoba is a delicious city in which to wander. In the narrow, whitewashed streets of the Juderia, wrought iron gateways give tantalizing glimpses of patios brimming with flowers. Delicious smells waft from courtyard restaurants where the deceptively strong Montilla wine, not unlike sherry, is served with your meal. An open air market now spreads across the Plaza de Corredera, where nobles on horseback used to fight bulls while the onlookers watched safely from the surrounding porticoes.

There are more statues to philosophers in Córdoba than anywhere else in Spain, a testament to its long-lost intellectual stature. But the strangest monument is the Tower of Malmuerta, built in 1404 by the Count of Priego as a penance for murdering his wife and two suspected lovers. The Count didn't stop at this but dealt swift justice to his butler, two maids and his pet parrot – presumably a talking one – for not informing him of the goings-on. All, it later transpired, were innocent, including the parrot.

Jealousy of a more constructive kind led to the creation of the Plaza Mayor, the magisterial square which is the heart of Madrid. When King Philip III of Spain saw Henry IV's new Place des Vosges in Paris in 1610, he compulsively ordered a bigger and better square for *his* capital. Over the years, the square witnessed stirring and sometimes sickening events. In 1622, more than 50,000 people watched the simultaneous canonization of five saints, Isidore, Ignatius Loyola, Francis Xavier, Felipe Nero and Teresa of Avila. The future King Charles I of England was guest of honour at an enormous celebration in the square when he came to court the Infanta Doña María, the 21 year-old sister of King Philip IV. Public executions were held here. And nobles dallied with their mistresses on the balconies: Philip VI had a special window-seat built for the actress, La Calderona, while gallants fought bulls from

horseback. In one squalid spectacle, the retarded Carlos II – known as The Bewitched – personally arranged for 120 condemned heretics to be publicly sentenced. The denunciation lasted 14 hours and, before a vast crowd, 101 of them were flogged and the rest despatched to the stake. Philip III's balcony on the Panadería, named after the old city bakery on the ground floor, was the place from which every subsequent King and Queen of Spain was proclaimed monarch, right until Isabel II, who was crowned in 1843 and exiled 25 years later.

From the **Plaza Mayor** (below) – now a sea of café tables – you walk through the Arch of the Knifemakers into ancient Madrid. Along the Cava Baja, lined with scruffy inns, dark and dingy shops

harbour potters, barrelmakers, woodturners and charcoal sellers. At the Hangman's Inn, a notice warns 'If you're drinking to forget, pay in advance' and in the Restaurant Botin the sucking-pig is so tender they carve it with the edge of a plate. On Sundays, the crowds jostle through the streets towards the Ribera de Curtidores, where the pavements are piled high with the mock antiques, secondhand throwouts and unashamed junk of the Madrid *Rastro*, or **flea market** (right). For a blissful hour, you can search for all those useless objects you have always wanted, wipe the dust from aged gramophone records, draw bows across dubious Stradivarii, have your misspelled name engraved on a brass plate, or haggle for a 'genuine' El Greco, painted only the day before.

A far more rewarding artistic experience is the Prado Museum, home of one of the finest art collections in the world. Its treasures galvanize the most blasé and footsore tourist. There is Leonardo da Vinci's second version of the Mona Lisa (superior to the one in the Louvre, say the Madrileños); and a room full of staggering Goyas, including the desperate *May 3, 1808* which – along with Guernica, by another Spaniard, Picasso – is one of the two most moving anti-war paintings ever created. There is Heironymus Bosch's terrifying vision of hell and damnation, *The Garden of Delight*; a wonderfully revealing self-portrait by Dürer and the masterwork of Velazquez, *Las Meninas* (*The Ladies in Waiting*). It is a painting you feel you can almost walk into. Its three-dimensional effect, its brilliant use of perspective and lighting – Velazquez incorporated himself into the composition – make it look more like a living stage-set than a painting. If you look closely, you will see a cross painted on Velazquez's tunic. It was added after the artist's death on the orders of a grief-stricken Philip IV to indicate that Velazquez, the official Court Painter, had finally been appointed a Knight of the Order of Santiago, an honour he had always craved. Legend has it that the cross was painted in by the King himself. One of the most striking pictures is Titian's portrait of Charles V, seated on a horse and wearing a spectacular suit of armour inlaid with gold, made to measure for the King in Augsburg in 1525. The actual suit of armour is preserved in one of Madrid's lesser-known museums, the Armoury adjoining the Royal Palace.

The priceless 'swordproof suitings' made for the kings of Spain are not displayed in conventional glass cases. They stand at the head of a huge 'army' of knights, footmen and magnificently caparisoned war horses. To walk into the Great Hall of the Armoury is to be confronted with a whole medieval battlefield on the march. There is armour not only for monarchs, men and mounts but even a pathetic little suit made for a royal child and an absurd set of armour plating for a pet dog.

In the Royal Armoury, you are surrounded by phantom soldiers. In the church of San Antonio de la Florida, you are embraced by the ghosts of Madrid's 18th century aristocracy. In 1798, Goya was commissioned to paint a fresco round the inside of the dome representing the Miracle of St Anthony. He painted an almost three-dimensional balcony, with a fashionably dressed throng of people peering over, strolling, chatting and laughing among themselves. To the embarrassment of the church, he used the faces of prominent courtiers and their mistresses, many of them well known courtesans of the time. From below, it appears as if they have all come out on the balcony to have a look at you – and the remains of their inspired creator. Goya's simple burial place is only a step away from your feet. His bones were brought back to Madrid from France after his death in 1828. However, there was one exception: they were unable to find his skull.

One of the reasons why Madrid superseded Toledo as Spain's capital was that Philip II wanted to be nearer his great project, the construction of the vast

and gloomy palace-mausoleum of **El Escorial** (left), 52 kilometres (32 miles) from the city. Built in the shape of a gridiron in memory of St Lawrence – who was supposed to have been roasted alive by the Romans – the Escorial contains 16 patios, 88 fountains, 13 chapels, nine towers, 15 cloisters, 86 stairways, 1,200 doors and 2,673 windows. The biggest building of its kind after the Vatican and the Kremlin, it cost the equivalent of £30,000,000.

As befitted a religious zealot, Philip's own private quarters consisted of a bare, cell-like room. In atrocious agony every step of the way, Philip was carried there to die in 1598. The journey from Madrid took a week. So ended the life of the austere, black-clad monarch who nearly became king of England. In 1554, Philip went to England to marry the devoutly Catholic Queen Mary, inspired by his father's plans to divide the two empires between the royal families. Everything depended on their being an heir. But Mary was in poor health and died, childless, four years later.

Philip married for the fourth and last time in 1570, again for political and dynastic reasons, taking as his Queen the youthful Anna of Austria. Disguised as a courtier, he caught his first glimpse of her in the less-than-austere surroundings of the 14th century **Alcázar of Segovia** (above): the palace-fortress which crowns the honey-coloured medley of churches, palaces, mansions and steep-stepped streets. Riding against the sky like an enchanted, fairytale castle, the Alcázar has also witnessed great and grave moments. King Alfonso X, who dabbled in astronomy,

propounded the then-heretical opinion that the earth revolved around the sun. The words were barely on paper before he was terrified by a thunderbolt, so apocalyptic that he immediately recanted. Isabella La Católica was living in the Alcázar when she was called upon to become Queen, the greatest in Spain's history. From one of the windows, the two-year-old Henry II of Trastamara fell to his death in 1366, followed by his nurse who committed suicide rather than face punishment. Prince Charles, later Charles I of England, was entertained here in 1623 and dined on 'certain trouts of extraordinary greatness'.

How the Prince responded to the 'extraordinary greatness' of Segovia's most massive monument is not recorded. The Roman Aqueduct, the largest and most complete piece of Roman building left in Spain, strides for 813 metres (889 yards) across the main square of the town like the legs of some gigantic column of legionaries. Beneath its 165 arches – some as high as 29 metres (94 feet) – the townsfolk scurry like ants; cars and buses become mere toys and even the houses which huddle against it look like building bricks left behind by some untidy child. Constructed without mortar, the aqueduct still carries Segovia's water supply, as it has for nearly 1900 years.

To the Moors, the most outrageous form of extravagance was to use water purely for pleasure and entertainment. At Granada in southern Spain, the **Alhambra** (below), the great palace conceived as Paradise on Earth by the Moors and built between the 13th and 14th centuries, seems to float on water. Its intricate wall carvings, like sheets of lace, are reflected in pools, basins and channels. Water spouts in delicate arcs from behind **groves of flowers** (inset), runs from the mouths of beasts, pirouettes from hidden fountains, even forms liquid handrails. The Alhambra is a magical oasis, a vast desert-tent turned into stone and plaster with slender columns in place of palm trees and delicate arches for fronds. The honeycomb ceilings are plaster beehives filled with light. The walls are lined with brilliant tiles whose intricate, mathematical patterns are so ingenious they seem to change, transform, regroup as you gaze at them. 'Allah is Conqueror!' runs the phrase in Arabic script which is endlessly repeated in plasterwork round the walls of the Alhambra Palace. Among the 124 pencil-thin marble columns in the Court of the Lions, the Sultans feasted and loved, surrounded by poets, musicians and acrobats. The favourites sat in the Harem eating rose-petal jam and serenaded by musicians who had been blinded to prevent them seeing the concubines and causing jealousy. Later, the Sultan would choose his favourite for the night by throwing her an apple. The 781 year-old Spanish Empire of the Moors finally shrunk to Granada and their rose-red palace on the hill above the River Darro. In their last sigh of decadence, they elevated sensuality to an art form.

On January 2, 1492, the water was finally turned off for the Moors by the Christian conquerors of Granada, Ferdinand and Isabella. When the last Sultan, Boabdil, handed over the Alhambra to Isabella before riding into exile, he wept and said, 'Here are the keys to Paradise'. He was still in tears when he looked back at the city for the last time from a point some way out. His mother gave him short shrift. 'Do not weep like a woman', she snapped, 'for what you could not defend as a man!' The spot is still known as the Gate of the Moor's Last Sigh.

THE COSTAS
& BEYOND

THIS is Spain's most familiar face – the great tourist coastline. A necklace of coves and beaches backed by rugged cliffs, rich, semi-tropical farmland or the winnowing foothills of the sierras. A beguiling decoration looped round the features of inland Spain. A short distance from the neon and the concrete, you enter a different world. The Costa Brava was one of the first areas to be developed, but it is still easy to find pockets of peace; in Aiguablava, for instance, and Cadaques, a village so perfect that artists almost outnumber the fishermen. It is the same on the islands. An old fashioned mountain railway will draw you away from the 20th century in Majorca. Ibiza is a composite of Mediterranean history and on Menorca, tiny details reflect a long-gone English way of life. Compared with the lively resort of Benidorm, on the Costa Blanca, Guadalest seems light-years away in time and atmosphere. The Costa del Sol, 130 kilometres (80 miles) of international playground, finds no echo in tranquil Frigiliana, a tiny mountain village barely seven kilometres (four miles) from the sea, where the last 'package tourists' were the invading Moors, many years ago. And where, when you buy a single stamp in one of the inky-dark shops, they meticulously wrap it up for you and bid you *Vaya con Dios*, 'God be with you', as you leave.

In the words of the old conundrum, when is a Spanish town not a Spanish town? The answer is Llivia, the first place you reach in Pyrenean Spain after the French frontier. Actually, you reach it *before* the frontier. It is one of those topographical oddities, a Spanish enclave five kilometres (three miles) inside France, connected by a road which is Spanish territory. Llivia was marooned in France because of the faultily worded Treaty of the Pyrenees in 1660, under which 33 villages were handed over to France. But Llivia had just been declared a township and insisted the Treaty did not apply. And so she has remained in Spanish hands; complete with picturesque alleys, fortified church and a pharmacy dating back to 1415, stuffed with medicine jars bearing the image of the Saint responsible for curing each particular ailment.

Forgotten Llivia is technically in the province of Gerona, whose shoreline is the far-from-forgotten Costa Brava. From the French border, a road like a knotted rope twists through forests of stripped cork-oaks, looking for all the world like men who have lost their trousers. Great headlands – Costa Brava means 'The Rugged Coast' – separate tiny coves where aquamarine water shimmers far below between the umbrella pines. The last of Spain's great invasions began here. The tourist invasion of the 'Costas'.

Tossa de Mar (preceding pages) has changed a lot since Ava Gardner and James Mason mooned round the village in the movie *Pandora and the Flying Dutchman*, and crowds of sightseers now disturb the goldfinches in the cypress trees above the Greco-

Roman city of Ampurias, whose treasures are still being unearthed from the sand-dunes. But jugs, pots and dishes are still piled on the pavements at the pottery centre of La Bisbal; few sandals scuff the dust under the Roman gateway to the walled village of Peratallada and it may be decades before the 2,000 year old ruins of Ullestret ever echo to the click of cameras. Seclusion is still here for those who seek it. There are more fishing boats than flushed bodies on the town beach at La Escala and for the really determined recluse there is Monells, an unspoiled 16th century village accessible only along a narrow track and across a footbridge.

Down through the Costa Dorada – where only a little way inland the 800 year old towers of Poblet Monastery cast their benign shadow across fields of rippling barley – the impregnable fortress of Peñíscola rises from the sea at the end of a narrow causeway. Early in the 15th century, the anti-Pope Pedro de Luna sought refuge here and, as Pope Benedict XIII, challenged the Vatican to disprove his title. Unflurried, Rome elected its own Pontiff (as it has done ever since) but Pedro gained enough support to sign documents founding St Andrew's University, in

Scotland, and, before his death in 1422, to name his successor. It is said – fancifully, I suspect – that Pedro's present-day descendant lives in secret somewhere in Spain, waiting for 'the call'. Who knows, he could be one of the strollers in the palm-lined Esplanade of nearby **Alicante** (above), his anti-Papal feet treading the pavement of wavy mosaic instead of the marble floors of St Peter's.

Behind the bright lights of **Benidorm** (right), one of Spain's most popular resorts, lies another anachronism. The sun-baked, Middle Eastern appearance of the town of Elche is only one reason why it has been called 'Spain's answer to Jerusalem'. For it stands in the centre of the biggest palm-forest outside Africa. An out-of-place oasis, where 125,000

palm trees arch over your head like cathedral vaulting. The oasis is not just cultivated for its dates but also for the five million palm fronds that are exported all over Spain and Europe to be used during the Palm Sunday services.

As if all that isn't enough, Almería even boasts 'Spain's answer to the Wild West'! The hills which enfold the city are as tawny and bare as an old blanket. But even in this Arizonan landscape, parched and gasping in 322 days of sunshine each year, you don't expect to blunder into Dodge City. Yet there it is, a plaster and plywood monument to the days when movie companies churned out cheap 'Garlic Westerns'. Once, it rattled to clenched words and quick triggers. Now you can walk up the main street, past the sheriff's office to the jailhouse, the stage-post and Madame Kitty's Select Saloon, without any gunslinger facing you out at high noon. The shooting is over. Both guns and cameras are silent. And the last coffin has gone to Boot Hill.

After Almería, the coast seems to plunge with a sigh of relief into more fertile countryside. The sparkling town of Almuñécar is surrounded by groves of avocado, oranges and grapefruit. From its dizzying peak, Salobreña Castle looks down on a straggle of cubist houses and a vast carpet of sugar cane whose stumps are burned at the end of the season by workmen who emerge sooty-faced from the smoke. The sugar-cane changes to acres of tomato plantations before Nerja, a miniature resort with a palm-shaded promenade that juts into the Mediterranean like the prow of a galleon. King Alfonso XII stood at the end of this promenade in 1885, gazed at the stirring views on either side and declared 'This is the balcony of Europe!' The name has been used ever since.

Incredibly, we have now come round to the Costa del Sol, the prototype of the 'Costa del Concrete' type of development which has turned much of the southern coastline into an architectural eulogy to the cement-mixer. But this is the lesser-known side, east

of Málaga, where the foothills of the sierras tumble down to the sea, breaking the coastline into hundreds of coves. A snaky coast road hugs the water's edge, past cheekily-painted fishing boats, drying nets, whitewashed huddles of fishermen's cottages and makeshift beach-bars where sardines are grilled on bamboo skewers over an open fire.

A line of crumbling watchtowers, the remains of coastal defences against the Barbary Pirates, runs ahead of you along the hilltops to Málaga, the bustling harbour-city which is visited by surprisingly few of the Costa del Sol's three million yearly visitors. Horse-drawn carriages clip-clop along the palm-shaded Paseo del Parque. The horses' heads are protected by little parasols or straw hats – a legacy from the days when wealthy Britons used to winter in Málaga and implacable old ladies devoted themselves to looking after the city's animals. Exotic black swans with cherry-red beaks paddle in lakes beneath the palm fronds while hawk-nosed gipsy women peddle garish shawls and bedspreads among the café tables. Between the old market and the Cathedral (begun in 1528 but with one tower still unfinished, as if to say 'How about that for *mañana*?') is the ancient quarter, where murky little bodegas sell the sweet Málaga wine straight from the barrel. High above the Cathedral and the city's Moorish Alcazaba fortress is the Parador-hotel of Gibralfaro, where you gaze down on what seems like a miniature port full of toy boats and a *plaza de toros* (a bullring) no bigger than a napkin ring. Away to the west curve the heat-hazed beaches of the real and unrepentant Costa del Sol, signalled by the beckoning concrete fingers of **Torremolinos** (left).

Lumbering moodily alongside the stretch of hectic highway and high-rise hotels are more mountain ranges: the Sierra de Mijas, the Sierra Blanca and the Sierra Bermeja. Cliffside villages like **Algotocin** (above) clutch at the rock face as if terrified of losing their foothold. Many of the towns here – Jimena, Chiclana, Arcos – have 'de la frontera' tacked on to their name, indicating they were once key frontier posts along the ever-changing battle lines between Christians and Moors. At the very tip of southern Spain, Tarifa is the nearest point to Africa. Broodingly Arabic in appearance and immured behind ochre walls, it seems never to have recovered from the shock of the Moorish invasion of 711. From one of its windows – during a siege in 1294 – Guzman the Good contemptuously threw his knife to the enemy so they could kill his son, held as a hostage, rather than surrender. When his own men cried in horror as the boy was killed, Guzman rushed to the battlements, then commented with arid stoicism, 'I feared for the moment that the infidel had gained the city'.

The Moorish arches of Tarifa are the gateway to Spain's least-visited coastline, the Costa de la Luz, where the Atlantic takes over from the Mediterranean and beaches the colour of doubloons are washed by the ocean tide. A clean, salty breeze strokes the face of Cadiz, Europe's oldest seaport.

Cadiz was founded in 1100 B.C. by the Phoenicians as a rival to Tartessos – known to the Bible as Tarshish – a long-lost city which is believed to have stood on the other side of the bay. 'Once in every three years', records the Bible, 'came the navy of Tarshish bringing gold, silver, ivory, apes and peacocks.' Cadiz, then called Gades, was soon competing with equally exotic exports. In Roman times, Cadiz was famous for its copper, wine, wool, salt fish and cocquettish dancing girls (*puellae Gaditanae*), a great attraction at Roman orgies. Cadiz has endured more than its fair share of disasters. In 1587, Sir Francis Drake sailed into the harbour and sank 33 ships of the Spanish fleet, an exploit which still inspires local mothers to warn their children, 'Drake will come and get you if you don't behave!' The real bogeyman, however, should have been the Earl of Essex, who 'singed the King of Spain's beard' in 1596 by destroying most of the old town, including the cathedral. A tidal wave engulfed Cadiz in 1755 and in 1800 the city shook under the bombardment of Admiral Nelson, who five years later met the combined Spanish and French fleets off Cape Trafalgar. The historic signal 'England expects every man to do his duty' was hoisted aboard Nelson's flagship and the French fired the first broadside. Barely five hours later, Napoleon's dream of invading England was over, Britain's naval supremacy was

firmly established and Nelson was dead. The French commander, Admiral Gravina, died in Cadiz of his wounds, commenting rather sportingly, 'I am going to join Nelson, the greatest man the world has ever produced'. It was only left to Napoleon to destroy some more of the city in 1810 and an ammunition explosion to wreak further havoc in 1947. One of the buildings which survived most of these catastrophes is the 17th Century church of St Catherine, which houses *The Mystical Betrothal of St Catherine*, undeniably the last painting by the Spanish artist, Murillo. While putting the finishing touches to the painting in 1682, Murillo slipped from the scaffolding and fell to his death on the altar.

Today, the old quarter of Cadiz is a jumble of cramped streets, strident with the sound of flamenco and full of *freidurias*, pokey bars ankle-deep in prawn shells where the locals munch through mounds of fried fish and shellfish and drink copious amounts of chilled sherry. The vine-shaded bodegas of **Jerez** (top left) – where millions of litres of sherry are stored in ecclesiastic gloom – are only 27 kilometres (17 miles) away. The Byass bodega alone holds 15 million litres and on one butt the artist Jean Cocteau wrote, 'Here I have drunk the blood of kings!' At the church of San Juan, built in 1423, a different sort of message was written in the blood of commoners. Trapped Christian soldiers used the blood from their wounds to write a desperate appeal for reinforcements.

Across the Guadalquivir river from Jerez is the loneliest place in Spain, the 250,000 acres of the Coto Doñana, a wildlife wilderness that is sanctuary for 135 species of birds and the last refuge in Europe of the pink flamingo. Pine-covered sand dunes melt into the marismas, the immense marshland tract of the Guadalquivir delta. Wild cattle and horses browse in the reeds, stags and wild boar crash through the undergrowth, spoonbill, heron and black kites wheel overhead. The lynx is the lord of the scrubland and the rare imperial eagle rules the skies, a predator so swift and terrible that the flamingo only has to see it approach to fold up her wings in panic, crash to the ground and die. In summer, the greatest danger is from vipers, who climb the trees to get away from the heat. Since the snakes hang from the branches, a man can be bitten on the head or throat, making the use of a tourniquet impossible.

Once more, the search for the 'real Spain' has ended in somewhere totally alien and unexpected. Yet **Frigiliana** (bottom left), a chalk-white village separated from the sea by carefully tilled and terraced fields, typical of the harmless indolence of Andalucia, bears no resemblance to the brutal beauty of the Coto Doñana, which dries out into a lifeless, arid steppe in summer. No 'family likeness' here to the medieval mysticism of Toledo or the rough-hewn heartiness of the Basque country; to the Oriental languor of Córdoba or the lofty piety of the Monastery of Montserrat, 48 kilometres (30 miles) from businesslike Barcelona. The monastery is part of the soul of Spain. It stands 1,190 metres (3,900 feet) high among a range of saw-toothed peaks. The setting is incomparable and the ancient legend that Montserrat was 'Monsalvat', the hiding place of the Holy Grail, inspired Wagner to compose his opera, *Parsifal*.

To Spain, Montserrat is sacred as the shrine of La Virgen Morena, the Black Virgin, a rather sinister image which is said to have been carved by St Luke. Young Catalan honeymooners traditionally visit the Virgin to ask her for blessing on their marriage and in the 14th century, Pedro IV of Aragón came to ask the Virgin to support his invasion of **Majorca** (preceding pages). From the peaks above the monastery, reached by funicular, the island is visible on a clear day, a whale-like mass floating far out in the Mediterranean. Now it is invaded by six million tourists each year, with, at the height of the season, 300 planeloads a day flying in and out of the only airport.

Nothing can ever equal that first, aerial view of Palma, the sugar-loaf bulk of the Cathedral rearing over the rooftops; even though you know that sunseekers lie shoulder-to-shoulder on the **beaches** (inset, previous page), packed as closely together as the masts of the yachts in the harbour. But Majorca is bigger than most people think: it covers 3,240 square kilometres (1,250 square miles) and has a backbone arching up to more than 1,220 metres (4,000 feet).

In a single day, you can drive round hairpin mountain passes with staggering views over the island, circle beautiful bays where fishermen are mending their nets as if posing for a photograph, pass hundreds of whitewashed windmills and roll through villages as somnolent as anything in Devon. There is an antiquated railway train which wheezes and clanks over the mountains, from Palma to Soller, passing through spectacular scenery. Huge, lonely crags rear overhead, while below you the ground falls away,

sweeping down to forests of pines, then fig and olive trees, finally flattening out to groves of oranges and almonds. Beyond lies the Mediterranean, as blue as a child's painting. Not all pleasures in Majorca are solitary. Every year, thousands of people who visit Lake Martel – deep in the bowels of the spectacular Caves of Drach – share one of the island's most magical moments. Suddenly, as if from another world, illuminated boats appear at the far edge, sailing towards you on the dark and mysterious water to the sound of the Barcarolle from Offenbach's *Tales of Hoffmann*. Nor is there any lack of company in Palma Cathedral, which was started in 1230 and not finished until 300 years later. I once saw pale Spanish toddlers being taught to genuflect, almost before they could walk, as the sun streamed through the immense, 1,236-piece kaleidoscope of the rose window, $12\frac{1}{2}$ metres (41 feet) wide and the largest in the world.

Although Menorca is the largest of the Balearic Islands after Majorca – roughly 48 kilometres (30 miles) long by 16 kilometres (10 miles) wide – it seems much smaller, an island in miniature. A few hills rise desultorily in the centre, but the main impression is of a flat, stony little place fighting a losing battle with the vegetation, like an overgrown rock-garden. The long years of English occupation – on and off from 1711 to 1802 – have left their mark: tall Georgian houses without balconies, sash windows, rocking chairs and Lord Nelson Gin, originally distilled to cater for the thirst of the British garrison. A British Governor, Sir Richard Kane, built the island's main road, which runs right down the centre linking Port

Mahon with the old capital, Ciudadela. There is no coastal road, so you have to take a 'herringbone' turn off the highway to reach **Cala de Santa Galdana**, (above), the horseshoe of sand with cream-coloured cliffs which many people believe is the finest beach in the Balearics. Although Ciudadela is no longer the capital – the British transferred the title to Port Mahon in 1722 because of its defensive superiority – it has never relinquished its dignity as the ecclesiastical and historic centre. Its 'high street' is the Mediterranean, the harbour reaching right into the centre of the town, past aristocratic 18th century mansions, cheerful cafés and the yachting quay, listed in the Blue Book of the Monaco Yacht Club, the sailing fraternity's 'Debrett'. Other vessels have not been quite so welcome as the luxury yachts. In the 16th and 17th centuries, Ciudadela was constantly attacked by Barbary Pirates and in 1558, the Turkish corsair Barbarossa almost destroyed the town.

Many of the pirate ships used the island-fortress of Ibiza as their base. So daring and confident were they, that they actually captured a British naval brig, the

Felicity, in 1806, looting her down to the last spar. **Ibiza Town** (left),buttressed by 16th century walls and rising straight from the sea, is an extraordinary layer-cake of civilizations. At the bottom is the Phoenician or Carthaginian layer (the world's finest collection of their art is in Ibiza's Archeological Museum), next come the Romans, followed by the Vandals, who mutilated their monuments. Higher up are the early Christian and Moorish layers and finally, like a cherry on the top, the massive belfry of the 13th century cathedral. Pouring down one side of the cake is the 'cream'; the Sa Penya quarter, a jumble of fishermen's houses built willy-nilly on the slope and glued together by whitewash. Superimposed, overlapping, piled on top of each other and playing architectural leapfrog, some actually block the narrow alleyways so that you have to edge round them on steps cut into the rock.

It is a long way from Spain, real or imagined. So far that the people of the Balearics refer offhandedly to the Spanish mainland as 'the peninsula'. They could be talking about Italy.

PEOPLE &
PASTIMES

THE Spanish have an infinite capacity for enjoying themselves, a quality which finds its greatest outlet at fiesta time. There are all kinds of fiestas for all the family, as at **Valencia** (preceding pages), each one revealing a separate facet of the Spanish character. The profound pageantry of the great Holy Week processions in Seville and Granada – where enormous religious floats are borne on the shoulders of the crowd and hooded penitents walk to the sound of muffled drums – are followed by weeks of uninhibited merriment. Spain is a nation of individualists and however spectacular the fiesta, there is always room for the individual gesture: the private patios so lovingly decorated in Córdoba; the elegant young horsemen of Jerez with their girlfriends riding behind them; the hair-raising bravado of the youths who run in front of the bulls at the Pamplona *encierro* or the bizarre moment in Málaga on Holy Wednesday when, by tradition, a single prisoner is chosen by lot and released from jail. The Spanish preoccupation with death, which reaches its climax in the ritual of the *Fiesta Brava*, the bullfight, does not prevent them from ending each day with a life-enhancing fiesta in miniature. Everyone puts on smart clothes and joins the *paseo* or evening stroll. It is the simplest fiesta of them all. And anyone can join in.

In Spain, history is something you can actually get your teeth into. The ancient Phoenicians brought the grape and the olive to Spain. The Moors constructed intricate irrigation systems which made citrus trees and market-gardens bloom and burgeon. The Discovery of America added tomatoes and green peppers to the Spanish table. And the giant prawns netted on the east coast can trace their 'family tree' back to around 240 B.C., when the first specimens were brought from Carthage by the warrior-king, Hasdrubal. Spanish cuisine is far more varied than most people think. There are fifty recognized ways of serving potatoes, for a start, and more than thirty different recipes for the delicious cold soup known as *gazpacho*. To walk into a big Spanish market is to enter a kind of gastronomic Aladdin's Cave, with the added advantage of being able to touch, prod, squeeze and sniff the produce in true Mediterranean fashion, before arguing about the weight with the **stallholder** (near right). There are red and green peppers like rugger balls, tomatoes as big as grapefruit, luscious figs, carrot-like radishes, pomegranates in pyramids and garlands of garlic. In the south, you'll find exotic fruit like *chirimoyas* ('custard apples'), with a flavour of lemon soufflé and salmon-pink *nisperas* (a form of apricot). Above open-fronted butchers' stalls, salamis, links of *chorizo* sausages, suckling pigs and giant *jamón serrano* hams hang in mouth-watering festoons. Even far from the sea, the fish is as fresh as the incoming tide. Refrigerated trains and lorries thunder through the night bringing **freshly-caught seafood** to the inland towns: hake, angler fish, sardines,

bonito, sole and mounds of flesh-pink prawns (far right). There are shellfish that will end up in that oddly-named dish, *zarzuela de mariscos*, the word *zarzuela* meaning 'comic opera', and unappetising looking crustaceans called *percebes*, which we call goose barnacles. They look like a monkey's finger and you strip off the gaiter-like covering to reveal the succulent flesh underneath.

According to connoisseurs, Spain is divided into five gourmet zones. The north – where the best food is to be found – is the area for sauces. The centre is roasting country, with suckling pig and baby lamb the great specialities. The south prides itself on fried food, while in the east the basis for many dishes is rice. And on the Ebro basin, the pot-roast meat in the rich and spicy *chilindron* sauce. They say the best paella – that savoury mixture of saffron rice packed with chicken, pepper and shellfish and served in a scalding iron dish – comes from Valencia. But my most memorable paella was made over an open fire on the beach at Nerja, in the Costa del Sol, by a rather eccentric restaurateur named Ayo. Every lunchtime during the summer, he cooks a monstrous paella for his customers, pouring in more than 16 kilos (35 lb) of shellfish, chicken and rice into a pan so vast that it takes three people to lift it.

Between meals, the Spanish are compulsive nibblers, aided and abetted by the long-standing tradition of *tapas*. These are little snacks served in almost every bar. Maybe just a sardine, a plate of olives or a slice of manchego cheese in the more modest places; but rising to elaborate dishes like mussels in white wine, deep-fried baby squid or *pinchitos moruños* – Moorish

Pins, or tiny kebabs – in the bigger and more expensive bars. Tapa is Spanish for 'lid' and the tradition started in the days when barmen covered each wineglass with a small plate, to stop anything falling in. Since the plate looked rather bare, they eventually added titbits as well.

The Spanish enjoyment of wine, however, goes back a lot further than the introduction of *tapas*. Two thousand years ago, Spanish vineyards were exporting so much wine to Rome that Italian growers – seeing their livelihood threatened – persuaded the authorities to limit the amount of new vines planted in Spain. Huge quantities were shipped to England as early as the 13th century and in the Canterbury Tales, Chaucer – no doubt speaking from experience – wrote

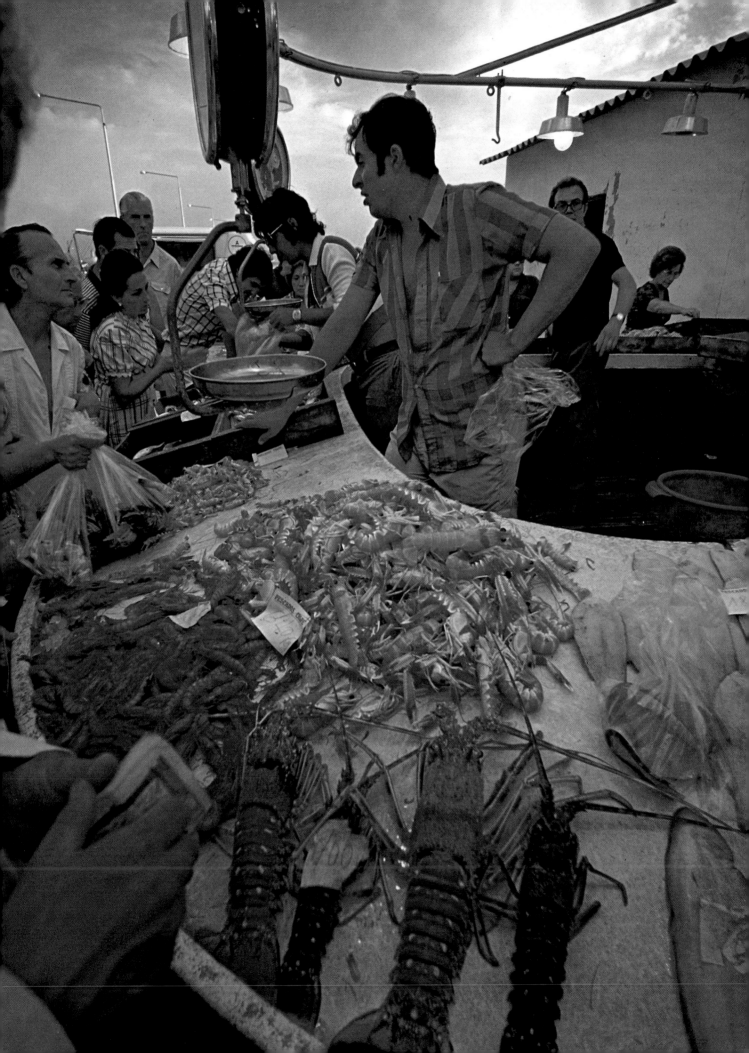

that 'this wine of Spaine creepeth subtilly'.
Tamburlaine – leader of the fierce Tartar hordes that
swept across eastern Europe in the 15th century –
enjoyed a glass of Málaga wine before massacres.
Catherine the Great of Russia preferred the red wine
of Navarre and the Emperor Charles V (Carlos I of
Spain) was so fond of Valdepenas that he carted large
quantities of it around on muleback during his
campaigns in the Low Countries. Of all the Spanish
wines, the most famous was sack, which later became
known as sherry because it was the nearest the
English could get to pronouncing Jerez, the name of
the town which is still the centre of the sherry
industry. Even now, Britain imports at least two
thirds of Spain's total sherry production of 50 million
litres. The grapes are still pressed by treading and in
cobwebby bodegas, the cellarman samples the wine by
pouring it from the barrel into a glass, using a **long-
handled dipper** known as a *venencia* (below). Visitors
are also able to sample the wines, as they can at San
Sadurni, near Barcelona, where most of Spain's
sparkling wine is produced. My fondest memory of
San Sadurni was of a couple of jovial young Irishmen
who tagged on to our party and proceeded to drink
the free bubbly as if they might never see the stuff
again. Eventually, I asked them where they were
spending their holiday. They weren't. They were
theological students training for the priesthood at a
nearby seminary and it was their afternoon off.

One only has to spend a short time in Spain to
realise that religion is a part of everyday life. The
result is an earthy, homespun piety that, to us,

sometimes appears almost irreverent. In Segovia
during the Civil War, the image of the Virgin at a
Carmelite convent was appointed Captain-General by
the Nationalist forces and still carries a field-
marshal's baton. While in a Socialist-held village, at
the same time, the Virgin was made a member of a
trade union to protect Her from desecration and was
issued with a membership card.

Religious fervour is stirred to its profoundest depths
in Spain during the Holy Week celebrations, when
cofradías, or brotherhoods, of devout Catholics carry
holy images through the streets on enormous floats,
their backs almost cracking under the strain. Their
lurching progress is accompanied by monotonous
drumbeats, the piercing cries of lone flamenco singers

and the tread of **hooded penitents** (far left) . . . images
straight from the Middle Ages. There are around sixty
cofradías in Seville – the longest single procession
lasts twelve hours – and some of them began in
unlikely ways. The *cofradía* of El Cachorro was named
after a 17th century flamenco singer, who was killed
in a knife fight, inspiring a sculptor who watched him
die to carve an agonizing image of the dying Christ.
And the gypsy *cofradía* of Los Negritos – the Little
Negroes – was founded in 1390 by the city's freed
black slaves, whose processions were so extravagant
and expensive that two of its members had to sell
themselves back into slavery to repay the debts.
Today, all 900 Negritos are white. In Málaga, when
the rival processions of Gypsies and Students meet at
one intersection, both sets of carriers must stand still
swaying the images on their shoulders till one of the
teams has to let theirs down from sheer exhaustion, or
until bowled over by the Spanish Foreign Legion, who
actually run with their patron, Cristo de la Buena
Muerte, while singing their lugubrious battle hymn, 'I
am the fiancé of Death'. But all is hushed on Good
Friday night during the procession of the Virgen de
Servitas, when all the lights are turned off and an
eerie silence descends on one of Spain's liveliest cities.

The eight-day festival of San Fermín in the northern
town of Pamplona is as bovine as Holy Week is divine.
Everything revolves round the ordeal of the *encierro*,
when the young men of Pamplona – augmented by
250,000 tourists from all over the world – run through
the **barricaded streets** in front of the bulls (above).
The daily *encierro* begins at eight in the morning and

the bulls, weighing around 500 kilos (1,100 lb) each, normally take only two and a half minutes to charge along the twisting, 890 metre (970 yard) route over slippery cobbles. It is a dangerous game, not helped by the two million litres of wine drunk during the celebrations. The idea is to keep ahead of the horns until the bulls reach the corralled bullring but every year produces its crop of casualties. In 1979, the 'score' was two men dead, 14 seriously injured and hundreds bruised and bleeding. No woman is ever hurt, for the simple reason that they are not allowed to take part. The bullfights that follow are often a disappointment, for after their ordeal in the streets the bulls are rarely in peak condition. And bullfighting is a serious, almost mystical affair; right from the moment the matador puts on his **'suit of lights'** (inset, previous page) to the final act of the bullfight when, alone, he has to dominate the bull with the small, red cape known as the **muleta** (previous page).

The British often refer to bullfighting as a sport. This is quite wrong, for nobody can 'win' in the conventional sense. It is a combination of ritual sacrifice and disciplined ballet, coupled with an exhibition of skill and bravery, presented in the form of a traditional spectacle. Basically a primitive tableau of man pitted against the forces of nature, it appeals to a fatalistic part of the Spanish character and it displays two of the qualities most highly regarded in a Spaniard: arrogance and courage. To understand the bullfight is to understand the Spanish. Bullfighters are the highest paid men in Spain. The

flamboyant El Cordobes earned £10,000 for each appearance and by the time he was 35, in 1971, he had a personal fortune of £12 million. But before you criticize them too severely for the part they play in this unarguably barbaric spectacle, remember they rarely retire. Many bullfighters die with their 'suit of lights' awash with blood and the screams of the crowd in their ears. Nearly 300 matadors have died in the ring this century. The greatest of them all, Manolete, was fatally gored when he turned his disdainful back on a bull he thought he had killed.

The bullfight is a climax to many of Spain's greatest fiestas, like the Seville feria, which follows Holy Week, when the city is thronged with families in Andalucian costume and the streets are lined with *casetas*, or marquees, where flamenco groups fight to make themselves heard over the joyous hubbub. But Spanish fiestas are as varied as its people and at the smaller, local affairs, one often feels that, at last, one is within reach of the essence of Spain.

In wine growing areas, everything leads up to the annual **harvest** (below left) and the blessing of the grapes in front of the church. Each Whitsun, 500,000 people converge on the lonely marshlands east of Huelva in a procession which trails across several provinces. They go to pay homage to the Virgin of El Rocio – known as La Paloma Blanca (the white dove) – with three days of singing, dancing and carousing. No such levity infects the celebrations at Caramiñal, near La Coruña, where villagers close to death have recovered after praying to the image of Christ. In gratitude, they walk through the village beside the coffins they would have filled, wearing the shrouds that would have covered them. At San Pedro Manrique, in June, young men walk barefoot – often carrying their girlfriends on their backs – across burning coals fifteen centimetres (six inches) deep, while in Valverde visitors witness the equally painful spectacle of 'The Impaled One'. A penitent, his identity concealed by a hood, is lashed tightly to a cross which he hauls round the village behind him. Many towns have mock battles between garishly-costumed Christians and Moors – recreating events which took place during the Reconquest – but only Pontevedra has the *rapa das bestas*. Scores of wild horses are rounded up in the mountains and herded into town, where young men leap astride them and symbolically cut their manes. And in Valencia, the fiesta really goes out with a bang as huge **papier-mâché figures** called *fallas* – usually illustrating a topical or satirical theme – are exploded in a welter of fireworks (right).

As the sounds of fiesta die away, we are still no nearer the real Spain. In a country so large, so diverse, so full of vivid contrasts, maybe there is no such thing. Is the real Spain an illusion and are we really searching for something inside *ourselves*? Caught up in the chant of 'Olé! Olé!' as a bullfight or flamenco performance reaches its emotional crescendo, it is easy to imagine that here is the true soul of Spain. But Olé is a corruption of the Arabic invocation 'Allah! Al-lah!', another echo from the shores of Islam. In the Land of Surprises, as the Spanish sometimes call their country, nothing is ever what it seems.

INDEX

(Figures in italics refer to illustrations)

Acknowledgements

The publishers would like to thank
the following organizations and
individuals for their kind permission to
reproduce the photographs in this book.
Adespoton Film Services 11 inset, 59
left; William Albert Allard/Image
Bank 17 right; Audio Impact/Stephen
Benson 30; Morton Beebe/Image Bank
32–33; Rainer Binder/Image Bank 52;
Robert Estall 12 right, 13, 14–15, 27,
31, 32 above, 45, 46, 53, 57; Gregory
Evans 34; Robert Golden 6–7; Alan
Hutchison 20–21, 26, 39 left;
Jaffry/Image Bank 58; N. Krieger/
Image Bank 60 inset; Robert
Lee/Image Bank 28–29; Toby
Molenaar 22 left, 35; Perrott Phillips
10, 11, 12 left, 16, 18, 22–23, 24–25, 40
inset, 47, 51 inset, 56, 60–61; Jurgen
Schmitt/Image Bank 4–5, 42–43, 50–51;
David Simson 17 left, 37, 54–55, 59;
Spectrum Colour Library 44; John
Lewis Stage/Image Bank 36, 40–41;
Ted Streshinsky/Image Bank 49
above, 62 left; Tovar/Image Bank
48–49; Luis Villota/Image Bank 1, 62
right; Zefa Picture Library/R. Everts
2–3, 8–9, 19, 38–39.

PDO 81-875